Blogging

The Super Simple Guide On How To Make Money Blogging in 2016

- Stop Working and Start Blogging-

by David Jones

Table of Contents

Disclaimer

While all attempts have been made to verify the information provided in this book, the author does not assume any responsibility for errors, omissions, or contrary interpretations of the subject matter contained within. The information provided in this book is for educational and entertainment purposes only. The reader is responsible for his or her own actions and the author does not accept any responsibilities for any liabilities or damages, real or perceived, resulting from the use of this information.

INTRODUCTION

Coming up with a blog that is going to move a large number of audiences and make you earn a lot of money is a no laughing matter. That is why I have decided to put together this guide, to help you make the choices which will increase your chances of developing a popular site that people will want to visit again and again.

This guide will hopefully give you some pointers, some tips and help you on your way to making your blog not only good, and read well, but also garner that all important traffic, fans, friends, commenters and possibly detractors and will eventually help you make lot of money.

This guide will show you how to monetize your blog, grabbing your share of traffic, which in turn will help make some revenue from your words. It will take you through the stages of setting up your blog, monetizing it and even how to drive traffic in easy to follow steps.

If you are new to blogging then I suggest you start at chapter one working your way through, however if you have already set up your blog and just looking to improve upon what you have already created, then pick and choose – dip in and out the parts that most benefit you.

You've probably heard all about blogging, vlogging, tweeting, podcasting, and microblogging, but might have assumed that becoming a blogger (someone who writes a blog), vlogger (someone who hosts/produces a video-based blog), and/or a podcaster (someone who produces an audio podcast) is too time consuming, too expensive, and wouldn't benefit you in any way.

Well, it is time that you should think about this over and over again.

In the past, if you wanted to reach a mass audience, it was necessary to land a job as a reporter for a major newspaper or magazine, or become the host of a radio or TV show.

Even if you managed to land one of these jobs, you still needed to adhere to the strict editorial guidelines of your bosses, and maintain a high level of journalistic integrity.

Thanks to blogging, however, anyone, from anywhere, has the ability to share their thoughts, ideas, knowledge, opinions, and/or expertise with a potentially vast worldwide audience, and the cost to do this is practically at lower cost.

Using a blog, it's possible to publish almost any type of content and make it available to the world within minutes—not hours, days, weeks, or months. Plus, thanks to the First Amendment, as a blogger, you're free to write or say just about anything, without having it edited or censored in any way. (Of course, slander, copyright infringement, and a few other laws still apply.)

But, for the most part, as a blogger, cyberspace is your stage, soapbox, or pulpit, and the millions of web surfers in the world are your potential audience members.

Some people create, publish, and manage a blog just for fun—as a way to share information with or entertain immediate friends and family. However, millions of other people have discovered that blogging is an extremely powerful and cost-effective marketing, promotional, sales, and advertising tool, if used correctly.

Using blogging as a powerful business tool is something that almost every business, in every industry, now needs to use to remain competitive.

This book will help you recognize and capitalize on the immense opportunity that awaits you. Blogging is a viable and accepted form of mass communication.

And, due to its low cost of entry, just about anybody can build a profitable business publishing blogs or incorporate a blog into their existing business's online activities.

Before we get started, the main idea you need to take away from this book is that, yes, blogging is easy to do. However, if you build it, they will not necessarily come. Even if you create and publish the most incredible, innovative, creative, imaginative, entertaining, informative, and engaging blog in the history of the internet, if you don't also invest the time and money necessary to promote your blog, it won't generate an audience.

After all, thousands of new blogs are created each and every day, and there are millions upon millions of successful (and not-so-successful) blogs already out there in the blogosphere.

If you want your blog to be successful, you'll need to be creative and innovative, target your original content directly to your intended audience, and most important, promote your blog to build and maintain its following.

Thus, the blogging process can be summed up using the following four steps, which we'll explore in detail throughout this book:

1. Create original blog content that's targeted to and will appeal to your intended audience. As you'll discover, your blog can include text, photos, video, active links, graphics, and other multimedia content.

2. Publish your blog, and make it available to the world.

3. Maintain your blog, and keep it updated with new and innovative content on an ongoing basis.

4. Promote your blog on an ongoing basis to establish, and then continuously build and maintain, its audience.

To become a successful blogger doesn't necessarily require a lot of money, but it does require dedication and the investment of time and resources. Unless you aggressively approach each of the four blogging steps just described, your blog will probably fail.

If, however, you take the right approach and go into this project with realistic expectations, the possibilities are truly limitless. Before we really get started learning all about blogging, it's important to understand that these days, a blog can take on many forms.

It can be created using just text, or you can combine text with photos, video, audio, computer graphics, and other multimedia content in order to convey your core message or information to your intended audience.

Likewise, a blog does not need to be a stand-alone entity. It can be published as part of a website or Facebook page, for example, or it can be directly linked to everything else you're doing online.

In the past, a blog was mainly text-based. Thanks to recent advancements in internet-related technologies, the line between blogging, vlogging, podcasting, website publishing, and being active on services like Facebook and Google+ has blurred. Thus, within this book, we'll touch on how to best utilize many of these technologies and methods for effectively reaching your target audience.

Based on what you're trying to accomplish, you may discover that just using text isn't the best way to communicate your core message, and that also utilizing photos allows you to more effectively reach your audience.

Or, you may want to invest in video production (for vlogging) or produce audio-based podcasts to communicate with your intended audience. Each of these communication methods relates to blogging, yet requires a different set of skills to create, plus can have a different impact on your audience.

If your goal is to generate revenue from your blog and develop yourself into an online celebrity or internet personality, this is the best book, to getting you going.

CHAPTER 1- UNDERSTANDING WHAT A BLOG IS

To start with, you should well understand what a blog is before you decide to venture into the business. By doing this, you will have the full information about what you are going to venture into.

First, think carefully about what you want to say and what information you want to communicate via your blog. Make sure you have enough content to share over the long term, and will be able to regularly update your blog with fresh, engaging, and relevant content.

Next, consider who your target audience will be. Then, figure out the best way to convey your information to your audience, and determine if you'll primarily use text, photos, video, audio, computer graphics, and/or other multi- media content.

Think about how much technological knowledge you have, and how much time and money you want to invest in developing and producing your content.

Once you've considered all of these important elements, you'll be in a much better position to begin planning and creating what will hopefully become a successful blog. Plus, you'll be able to determine which service you'll use to host your blog, and be able to discover effective ways to promote it.

This book will help you understand the significance of the blogging phenomenon, and more importantly, show you how people from around the world are using blogging to circumvent commonly accepted publishing procedures, and keep the profits generated from their own work, while also maintaining 100 percent creative control over their content.

Once you decide to create a blog, the next step is to come up with an amazing topic to write about—one that will allow you to keep creating new, interesting, engaging, and innovative content (blog entries) on an ongoing basis.

Once you've chosen your topic, it's important to develop an overall goal for your blog. You must truly understand the blog's purpose and what you want to get out of it. At the same time, you need to clearly define your blog's target audience, then develop content that caters specifically to that audience. All this needs to be part of your blog planning process, but more on that later.

As with any business, success is impossible without a solid foundation.

Take your time with each and every step. Do your research, and think about the long-term ramifications of everything you do. At the same time, keep considering your overall blogging objectives, and make sure your actions will help you achieve them.

While there's no limit to how much money you can earn running a successful and popular blog, it's important to have realistic expectations. Truly successful bloggers often use their blog as a way to better communicate with customers and clients, or as a sales and marketing tool for their businesses.

If you're creating a blog as a business venture with hopes it will generate profits, this requires a lot of planning and promotion, because you'll need to build and maintain an extremely large and dedicated following for the blog before it will generate any serious revenue.

In fact, self-publishing and self-promoting any type of work can be a bit of a challenge. While it won't cost you a fortune to create and publish a successful blog that generates revenue, it will require that you put in serious work—not just creating, publishing, managing, and promoting the blog, but also over-seeing the business side of the online venture as well.

Before you start calculating all the riches you'll be earning as a blogger, let's spend a few minutes exploring what a blog, vlog, podcast, and microblog actually are. After all, you need to determine if this is what you want to do, what approach you want to take, and whether you have the wherewithal to do it right.

Let's first start by knowing what a blog means

WHAT IS A BLOG?

The term "blog" comes from combining the words "web" and "log," which was used for a short time to describe websites that published a running archive of dated entries, sort of like a digital diary that was displayed in chronological order. The techno-geeks that created the first "web logs" coined the term "weblog," which ultimately evolved into the term "blog."

The word "blog," as a noun, can describe a regularly updated, primarily text- based website with individual, dated posts that are displayed chronologically.

This is a traditional blog. Of course, today's traditional blogs can also incorporate photos, videos, audio, and graphics, but they're primarily text-based, and use a standard format for each entry.

The word can also be used as a verb, as in "to blog," meaning to actively submit posts to a website, which is also referred to as "blogging." The people who run blogs are known as "bloggers," and the whole collection of all the internet's blogs is known as the "blogosphere."

The anatomy of a traditional, text-based blog is nothing more than a basic website with a bunch of dated entries. All of the blogging services that host blogs allow bloggers to customize the look of their blog, by choosing text colors, fonts, and an overall layout or design.

Many use professionally created templates that can be fully customized but that require no programming to use.

Beyond traditional blogs, there are also vlogs, podcasts, and microblogs. A vlog is a collection of videos, recorded and edited by the vlogger.

Instead of using text, the vlogger stars in their own videos, and often simply looks into the camera and talks to their audience. You'll find many popular vloggers on YouTube. Some have become popular internet personalities with huge followings.

Thanks to Twitter, and services like Facebook and Google+, millions of people have gotten hooked on microblogging.

Instead of writing lots of text for a traditional blog, or recording videos for a vlog, they simply update their microblog feed with ongoing entries which are no longer than 140 characters in length (about one sentence long).

Meanwhile, for people who don't like to write, services like Instagram allow people to upload images and include an optional text-based caption, keywords, and location to a photo.

For obvious reasons, microblogging is the easiest to do and requires the least amount of time and effort. Yet there are microbloggers with millions of followers who use their Twitter feed, for example, to promote their company, products, services, or themselves very successfully.

Many individuals as well as companies often use a combination of online activities to achieve their goals. For example, they'd use a blog to promote a company, product, or service's website, and then use a Twitter feed and/or a Facebook page to promote the blog and/or the website.

YouTube videos can also be used to cross-promote a website, blog, Facebook page, and/or Twitter feed. Thus, the same core content and message is repackaged in several ways, across multiple platforms, to reach a broader audience using different forms of media.

There are no limits as to what topic can be covered within a blog. You can convey thoughts, ideas, facts, or opinions. You can also offer how-to information, share your expertise, spread gossip, or promote a person, company, product, or service. Some blogs are created just for fun—to make people laugh or to share information with friends and immediate family.

These blogs cover topics such as how to build websites, what technologies to try, and what up-and-coming trends to watch. These bloggers alert their audience to exciting news by keeping a constant finger on the pulse of a particular industry, and provide a valuable service.

CHAPTER 2- PLANNING AND CREATING YOUR BLOG

A blog can be about anything, but to be successful, a blog must provide a valuable and tangible service or benefit to its readers. The content you create needs to be informative, entertaining, unique, creative, and/or engaging—something people want to read or watch.

It also needs to be consistent. Blogs that aren't well focused find it very difficult to find and then retain an audience.

You should be certain that your blog, and your chosen topic, provide valuable and informative content. After all, if you're able to provide valuable and reliable content of any kind, you'll develop an audience, and that audience can keep growing.

Blogging is a fast-growing phenomenon. As blogging becomes even more mainstream and widespread, so does your potential audience. Blogs can be accessed from a desktop or notebook computer, any wireless internet device, an interactive TV set, a tablet (such as the iPad), or even a smartphone.

So as more individuals, companies, and organizations use blogs to communicate, more people will devote their time to reading blogs.

Without a doubt, blogging will continue to become more popular and evolve in the next years. It's not too late to jump on the bandwagon and become a successful blogger.

Even if you can't come up with something truly unique to blog about, you can still develop a new twist to present your content and take a new approach when it comes to presenting it to your targeted audience.

With your enthusiasm to explore the world of professional blogging, and the tools and information provided in this informative book, you'll potentially be able to earn money running a blog.

The amount of money you earn will be up to you. Keep in mind, many companies currently use a blog as a sales, marketing, promotional, or advertising tool, and/or to enhance their customer service or technical support. The blog can be used to generate revenue.

It All Starts with a Great Idea

As you already know, one of the first steps for launching a successful blog is the planning phase. Just as you wouldn't launch a company without a detailed business plan, you don't want to simply create a blog without a plan, especially if you're hoping to generate revenue from it or use the blog in conjunction with your existing business.

This section covers the things you'll need to anticipate and the preparations you'll want to make before ever touching your keyboard to create your first blog entry.

A successful blog must have four main features:

1. A steady stream of original, interesting, informative, engaging, and/or entertaining content. The content should be targeted to its audience and displayed or presented in a way that's easy to read and visually appealing.

2. A large and ever-growing audience

3. One or more reliable revenue sources (if the goal of the blog is, in fact, to generate revenue)

4. It should be synergistic with all of your other online activities, including what you do via your website, Facebook page, Twitter feed, and/or YouTube channel, etc.

Choosing a Profitable Topic

One of the most crucial and essential parts in creating and planning your blog is choosing a topic that will generate you good cash. When it comes to selecting an outstanding topic that will generate more profits and make you have a large number of audiences, you will need to have many factors to consider.

Things such as topic know how, the interest of the audiences and you competitors tactics should be considered before coming up with a topic. As a blogger, you should always come up with unique ideas to help you outdo your competitors in the market.

Here are some of the factors you should consider.

1) The audience targeted- The content that you are going to write should aim at a particular audience

2) Are you targeting a large audience? – You should consider how you are going to reach and inform your intended audience about the blog.

3) Is the topic you are choosing have more to write in the future?

4) Does the topic have many competitors in the market?

5) Which measures are you going to take to make your topic unique and different from other competitors?

If your goal is to attract millions of visitors every month to a blog, the topic you select should have mass appeal or be somewhat mainstream, yet have a unique twist to it. As you try to determine the size of your audience, be realistic and develop appropriate expectations.

For example, a blog that addresses the political happenings in your town of 30,000 people may very well become the hottest thing in that town, but the audience growth potential has a ceiling. People in other towns, much less in other states or countries, will have little or no interest in your blog.

Even if you create the most incredible blog and the potential audience is the people in your town, realistically, it's likely that only one out of every 10 people in your town will have the time or interest to read blogs in the course of their day, and of those few people, even fewer are most likely interested in local politics.

So while the topic of local politics may excite you personally, the reality is that this topic is very limited in terms of its potential audience and ability to grow.

Bloggers just like you have achieved success blogging about a wide range of topics. The following are just a few general areas that you might consider as you choose what you'll blog about.

If you're operating a blog for a company, the blog itself can focus on your company, its philosophies, and/or the people who run the company, for example. The blog can (and should) be targeted to your potential and/or existing customers or clients.

Consider using a company blog to explain how to best use your product or service (i.e., provide step-by-step how-to information), share customer testimonials, offer product comparisons, and/or interact with your customers in an informal way in order to share new information about products/services on the horizon.

If you're at a loss for words but have photos that can tell a story, consider creating a photo blog or using a service like Facebook, Google+, Instagram, or Pinterest to share your digital images. Just as with traditional blogs, there are no rules for creating photo blogs and/or online galleries, so you can opt to include a detailed photo caption for each image, or allow each photo to speak for itself.

Photos displayed in a pre-determined sequence, for example, can be used to tell a powerful story. It's also possible to publish exactly where and when each photo was taken, and link keywords or tags to each photo, which make it easier for people to find.

Industry-Oriented Topics

One way to virtually ensure you'll have plenty to blog about, now and in the future, is to focus on a specific industry and blog about that industry as a whole. For example, there's the "entertainment industry," or more specifically, "TV," "music," "movies," or "celebrities."

There's also the computer industry, consumer electronics, sports, fashion, mining, transportation, and literally thousands of other potential industries to choose from, provided you have some knowledge about the industry and something to say in your blog.

Within a single industry, there are probably thousands or even tens of thousands or millions of people who work within it. These would be potential audience members for your blog, as would be consumers who benefit from the products or services created by your choice of industries to blog about.

Once you have a general industry or topic, try to narrow it down a bit so the blog will have focus and appeal to a specific group of people.

Blogs about commodity items, such as digital cameras and consumer electronics, for example, provide good advertising options for bloggers and can potentially offer a stable source of advertising revenue.

If you choose to cover the technology industry, you'll quickly find you have some significant competition. Do some researches before you launch your blog. Find out what's out there, and discover a way to do it better, or focus on a different niche to cover.

There are plenty of niches within the tech industry, or any industry for that matter, that you can choose from and potentially offer a blog with a unique perspective.

As you consider all of the thousands of different industries out there, you'll certainly be able to find at least one that appeal to you and that you'd have an interest in blogging about.

If you choose to blog about an industry, much of your time preparing content (blog entries) will be spent searching for industry news, following industry trends, reporting about industry breakthroughs, and discussing industry gossip.

Blogs Focusing on an Organization

Once your blog is published, you'll need to promote it to all your social networks. The fastest, easiest, and most cost-effective way to quickly build an audience is to generate positive word-of-mouth about your blog.

Encourage your blog's followers to tell their friends about it. Publish a "Share" button or "Share" icons with each blog entry—it's free, easy, and powerful.

Posting personal artwork, such as drawings, paintings, or photography, has helped some bloggers not only earn money from art sales and related merchandising, but also gain fans and a dedicated following for their work.

Thousands of followers or fans gives you, the artist, added credibility and improves your real-world marketability. A popular art blog, for example, can lead to larger licensing, merchandising, or sponsorship deals.

Continuous Stream of Content

When choosing what to blog about, remember to choose an overall topic that won't dry up. Public interest is fickle and rarely stays on one topic for very long. So be sure to choose a topic that has held public interest (or the interest of your target audience) for a long time and will continue to do so in the future.

No one can control public interest. People can only influence public interest and trends, both of which can be somewhat predictable. Examine trends in the past, stick to reliable topics, and don't select a subject so esoteric that you limit your audience as you choose the focus on your blog.

As you develop your content, keep in mind that the attention span of your audience is very short. For text-based blogs, keep your postings short. Likewise, a video published within a blog or on YouTube, for example, should be kept to between three and five minutes in length.

Your Credibility as a Blogger

Choosing a topic that you are familiar is an ideal idea. You shouldn't choose a topic that you know little or nothing about.

Chances are, if you know nothing about the topic you select now, you don't have too much interest in the subject.

Ideally, you want to be absolutely passionate about whatever it is you blog about since that passion will come across to your audience. Plus, in the weeks and months to come, if you have a passion for your blogging topic, you'll enjoy the whole blogging process that much more.

If you can't honestly call yourself an expert in the topic you choose, get up to speed quickly by reading books, magazines, newspapers, and other blogs. To establish credibility, you'll want to choose a topic that isn't so large that your expertise doesn't seem plausible.

Choose a topic of manageable size and that can be used to enhance your credibility.

Existing Competition

Before you take on all of your competition in cyberspace, find out who that competition is and how much of it actually exists.

You'll do yourself a disservice by entering a topic area that's already chock-full of bloggers, unless you've developed a unique approach.

Similarly, taking on established industry experts can be prohibitively difficult, unless your qualifications are top-notch, and again, you have a different approach to creating your content.

You shouldn't completely disregard your chosen topic if you find that it's crowded or well-covered. While that may be what you end up doing, you should consider adjusting your tactics first.

If your preferred topic is crowded, readership for that type of content may already be spread too thin across too many blogs (and other media outlets), thereby leaving all the blogs with little traffic or profit potential.

As you study your competition, take detailed notes in regard to how and where other people are succeeding and where they're falling behind. Learn specifically what works (in terms of your blog topic and its target audience) and improve upon or fix what doesn't. In other words, learn from your competitors' mistakes and don't try to reinvent the wheel.

Your Interest and Passion

Before committing yourself to one particular topic, realize that whatever topic you choose will become the focal point of your everyday blogging life.

Consider this carefully and objectively. You don't want to be stuck with a blog you can't stand, and ultimately, a job that you hate or resent. Remember, you're potentially starting a moneymaking blogging "business," which means taking the project beyond where a mere hobbyist would go.

When people read your blog content, it should become immediately obvious that not only are you an expert on the subject matter but you're also passionate about it. At the same time, it's essential that the blog's readers/viewers feel as if you're committed to them and to meeting all of their needs, wants, and interests as they're related to the topic.

Choose the Best Way to Present Your Content

When you're creating a traditional blog, the primary way you'll present your content is through the written word. However, don't forget you can also easily incorporate photos, graphs, charts, illustrations, animated graphics, digital slides, tables, music, audio, video, and other multimedia content in order to get your point across and convey your information.

Choose the method that best caters to your target audience, keeping in mind its attention span is very short. Then, once you choose the best method for communicating what you have to say, focus on the best way to say it. For example, research shows that people love to read top-10 lists as well as bulleted points that break up information into small chunks, making it easier to understand and digest.

That old saying that "a picture is worth a thousand words" is certainly true. Instead of wasting several paragraphs describing something, can you convey the same information using a single digital image, chart, or graph?

Deciding how to best communicate information within your blog is where knowing and understanding your audience, as well as creativity, come into play. While it's always good to incorporate one or more photos into a blog post to break up the text, only use images that are directly relevant to your content.

Avoid unnecessary distractions that will clutter the screen, and of course, make sure you have permission to use whatever photos or artwork you want to feature within your blog so you don't violate anyone else's copyrights or trademarks.

Create a Posting Schedule and Stick to It

Once you commit to becoming a blogger, figure out how often you'll publish new posts, and promote your schedule to your audience. Then, make sure you stick to that schedule. Failing to adhere to a regular posting schedule will make it very difficult to build and then retain an audience.

Before committing to a schedule, make sure you have enough content to meet that schedule over the long term. If you publish new postings daily, you don't want to run out of fresh ideas after a few weeks or months.

Even if you publish a new post once every two weeks or once a month, that's fine as long as that's what your audience expects, although frequency and consistency will allow you to grow your audience much faster.

Selecting a Blog Name

Selecting a suitable name for your blog is one of the more creative steps as you get started. Your blog's name should be creative, memorable, intriguing, and quickly summarize what your blog is all about and who it's of interest to. It will be how people find and recognize you.

When naming your blog, there are a few guidelines you should follow. First, create a descriptive name that's appropriate for your blog topic.

Domain Name Concerns

Keep your site's domain name in mind when naming your blog. Ideally, your blog's name should be your blog's domain name to keep things simple for your readers. Therefore, you should choose a brief and memorable name that works well with ".com" tagged onto the end of it.

Strategies for Producing Quality Videos (Vlogs)

When it comes to producing video-based content these days, you'll definitely want to utilize a camera capable of shooting high-definition (HD) quality video and take advantage of a camera that allows you to connect an external micro- phone so you can capture professional-quality audio.

This is particularly important if you're creating video content on behalf of a business that needs to maintain a professional reputation.

Choosing a Platform for Growth

Now that a few of the intangibles are out of the way, it's time to start planning the logistical aspects of getting your blog up and running. There are countless options when it comes to blog creation and hosting services, and to cover them all in one book isn't plausible, especially since new blogging services and technologies are constantly being introduced.

Hosted Blogging Services vs. Installed Server Applications

There are two main types of blogging platforms: hosted services and server applications. Both perform basically the same task of publishing a blog. Chances are, as you get started, any option you choose will meet your needs for creating a basic, straightforward, traditional, text-based blog.

However, if you want to add specialized functionality, interactivity, or unique features to your blog, you'll want to pay careful attention to what's offered by each type of service or software product.

There are significant technological differences between hosted blogging services and installed server applications. The method you choose will have a significant impact on how you run your blog in the future, as well as on your operational costs.

Hosted Blogging Services

A hosted blogging service is an entirely web-based option for publishing a blog. All aspects of your blog's creation, publishing, and management are done online, using online-based tools. All you need is access to the web from any standard internet browser (or a specialized app on your tablet or smartphone).

All your interactions with the blogging service, including setting up and the posting of new entries to your own blog, is done through the blogging service's website.

There's nothing to download or install, no programming is required, and you can begin blogging immediately. This is also a very low-cost option. In fact, many of the hosted blogging services are free of charge.

To first establish your blog, you'll need to choose a blog hosting service, and then register with that service. This process takes no more than a few minutes.

To register initially, you'll need to supply basic information about yourself, including your name and email address.

Once registered, you're given a web address URL for your blog. Your blog's address, at least initially, will be some extension of the blogging service's address. Some services allow you to choose this extension, and some assign it to you. Your new blog's address could take any of several different formats.

To make things easy for your followers, ultimately what you'll want to do is register an easy-to-remember domain name, and then forward it to your assigned blog address.

Suitability for Your Content

When researching the various blogging platforms, be sure to consider your intended content. In terms of storage, functionality, and bandwidth, for example, your needs will be vastly different if you'll be operating a traditional text- based blog versus publishing podcasts or videos.

All the traffic analysis and ad network integration in the world won't help you if the service doesn't allow you to post photos on your photo blog. The first thing to look for in a blogging service or application is the ability to handle the content you wish to include within your blog.

In some cases, a blog is comprised simply of text, hyperlinks, and photos. To meet the needs of this type of blog, any blog service you choose will be able to handle all the content you need.

But as the blogging phenomenon has expanded, so have the requirements of the bloggers. To keep up with the competition, you may need your blog to play audio clips, videos, Flash animations, or have some level of interactivity. Be sure to check out the feature lists of each blog platform.

Advertising Capacity

Depending on the goals of your blog, you may choose to generate revenue from it by displaying ads from other companies. Most of the blogging services have built-in advertising capabilities, plus the ability to quickly integrate Google AdSense ads or other forms of display or search advertising ads.

This functionality makes generating revenue by displaying ads relatively easy, assuming your blog receives significant traffic and the displayed ads interest your blog's audience. Popular ad networks, such as Google's AdSense, sometimes affiliate themselves with a particular blogging service to enable users of that service to install their ads in a few steps.

Once your blog begins drawing serious traffic, you may outgrow Google Ad- Sense advertising, and depending on the blog service you ultimately use, incorporating other outside ad networks may not be allowed or technically possible.

There may come a time in your blogging life when you'll want to solicit individual advertisers and/or belong to multiple ad networks. Therefore, you Should find a blogging service that not only makes advertising easy in the beginning but also allows for expansion. Ask the blog service providers if they lock you into a single ad network and if they allow access to your blog's template code for more ad integration later.

CHAPTER 3- PUBLISHING YOUR BLOG

When it comes to publishing your blog content, there are literally hundreds of applications and online-based hosting services you can choose from. They range in price from free to charging a certain hosting fee per month, depending on your needs. Some are well-known, owned and operated by huge online companies, like Google, while others are much smaller operations.

There are many books, websites, and even other blogs devoted to helping first-time users get set up with each of the popular services and applications. Also, each service typically provides extensive instructions for getting started.

Because each offers a different array of services, features, and functionality, your best bet is to carefully define your needs first (based on the goals for your blog or vlog), then contact each service's website or technical support department to learn about the latest feature offerings, and for instructions on how to begin using their respective service or application.

Consider Hiring a Freelancer to Help You Get Started

If you have no graphic design or website design experience, consider hiring a freelancer to help you initially set up your blog and then customize a blog template for you. This also applies to branding and customizing a YouTube channel.

Working with a freelancer initially will help to ensure everything gets set up correctly and that you launch your blog with a unique and personalized appearance (layout and design) that's based on your specific needs and that will appeal to your target audience.

No matter which blogging service you ultimately use, once the blog is set up and the template you choose has been customized, as the blogger, you can then create and publish new posts to the blog easily and from virtually anywhere that includes text, photos, and/or video using a computer, tablet, or smartphone.

While a freelancer with expertise in graphic design or website design can initially be used to help you get started, based on your skills as a writer, you might also consider hiring a freelance editor to edit your blog posts before they're published. This will ensure the content is free of spelling and grammatical errors and that it's easily readable using language that caters to your audience.

It's essential that your blog convey a sense of professionalism in order for you to build up credibility as a blogger and to build and/or maintain the reputation of the company the blog will be representing.

Thus, the blog's layout and design should look professional, and the content should be well-written and free of errors. You also want to make sure that it conveys the right attitude and is properly branded.

Likewise, if you plan to incorporate illustrations, artwork, computer graphics, photography, or video into your blog, you can hire freelancers who can inexpensively create this content from scratch. This will help to ensure your blog's content is unique and that you don't accidentally violate anyone else's copyrights by using content that doesn't belong to you.

Community Blogging Services

As blogging continues to grow in popularity, many online social networking sites that originally didn't offer blogging services have begun to do so. For example, anyone can create a blog for free using a personal Facebook page or create a separate Facebook page for their company, group, or organization.

If you use a service like Facebook as your primary blogging platform, keep in mind your options for displaying ads in conjunction with your blog are limited to the opportunities Facebook offers.

Your ability to directly sell themed merchandise or products through a Facebook page is also limited. Yet, Facebook does offer a robust set of tools for creating a personal or company Facebook page that allows you to maintain a blog and then utilize Facebook's free and fee-based tools for attracting followers to it.

Regardless of which service you use to host your blog, when it comes time to promoting it and building your audience, you'll definitely want to utilize Facebook, Twitter, and the other popular online social networking services.

Anyone can design, create, and publish a free blog using a service like Blog- ger.com very quickly.

However, if the features offered by this or a similar service, combined with the widgets available for the blogging platform, aren't customizable or robust enough to meet your needs, consider using one of the more advanced blogging services, such as WordPress.com (which ultimately requires more of a learning curve from the blogger's standpoint, due to its more advanced and customizable features).

CHAPTER 4- PROMOTING YOUR BLOG AND BUILDING YOUR AUDIENCE

Always remember that sustainable blog traffic growth can only happen if your content rocks. Having somebody visit your blog once is just one thing – but having them to come back again and again is another and that is the reason why awesome content is a necessity if you want to profit from your blog.

The process for generating profits from a blog isn't always easy, but the first step is to build a massive and loyal audience/following.

The best approach to achieve this isn't always clear, and the strategies needed to achieve this goal are different for everyone, depending on the type of blog they're creating, who the target audience is, what the goal of the blog is, and how well the blogger (that's you) manages to promote their blog.

Building, maintaining, and constantly expanding your blog's following (audience) is an absolute requirement if you ultimately want to generate revenue from your blog.

Of course, if you chose a topic you're passionate about to be the main focus of your blog, the hard work you'll need to put in while building your blogging business won't always seem like work. Here are some of the ways to build traffic on your blog:

Create an Identifiable Logo for Your Blog

Develop your blog into an identifiable brand. If you're starting a blog from scratch, consider having a unique logo designed for it, and begin to develop an entire brand and visual identity around the blog. Or, if you're developing a blog for your company, incorporate your existing logo, branding, and slogans, for example, to maintain continuity.

WORD OF MOUTH

Word of mouth is a great way to start building traffic on your blog – you tell your friends about your blog, who in turn tell their family and friends and that is how your list of readers increases – in case your content is read worthy.

Before you begin talking to people about your blog, spend some time crafting your elevator pitch. This is a thirty second overview of what your blog is about and how readers can benefit from it. Once you are ready with the pitch, practice it, hone it and own it.

Here are some ideas about how to build word of mouth publicity for your blog:

COMMENTING ON OTHER BLOGS

A better approach here is to read the blogs that you like –
especially the ones that you feel have a great crossover traffic –
and leave a thoughtful comment with your blog URL only if
you genuinely have to say something. This means that your
comments have to be genuine, straight from your heart. If
your comments are genuine and insightful, they may lead
other readers from the blog to reach out to you via your blog.

PROMOTE OTHER BLOGS

Promoting another blogger can be as simple as linking back to
another blogger whose post inspired any of your posts. Most
blogs have trackbacks on their blog posts – this means that if
you link a person's blog, they will automatically get a
notification that you linked their blog.

NETWORKING

Networking can open new doors for your blogging business. Apart from forging genuine friendships, you get the opportunity to grow your blog. I must mention here that 'true, genuine friendships' come first. If you make friends with the intention of growing your business, your friends can see right through your eyes.

The best way to connect with other bloggers is via blog conferences. This is a highly misunderstood profession and I can't tell you how amazing it is to be in the company of like-minded people who understand what you do for a living.

GUEST POSTS

Guest posts have an amazing potential to drive traffic to your own blog. The key to a great guest post is to not post on a site with a similar audience but to write something so great that your host's readers are driven to your site in order to read more of what you write.

If you are interested in guest posting on other sites, make sure that you ask for guidelines and always submit original content. Also, do not try to be overly familiar – since this is not 'your' audience. You are writing for somebody else's audience.

Submit your best content and never make your post self-promotional.

BUILD YOUR E MAIL LIST

'Building an email list' model is extremely impactful when you want to reach out to an audience that can be converted into a sales funnel that you want to use in order to sell your expensive courses or physical products. This model is extremely effective for online marketers.

As you build your email list, remember to place the subscribe button at a prominent place in your blog. Create some nice freebies for your subscribers – these could range from recipe books to goal setting and time management guides – just make sure that you are adding value to your readers. Always promote the incentive that you offer on social media

UNDERSTAND SEARCH ENGINE OPTIMIZATION

As you create content, remember to create content that is SEO friendly. You must remember that Google's only goal is to display the best possible content for a particular search. The extremely sophisticated Google algorithms look at everything ranging from the content on the web page to the time visitors spent on the page. Another important thing to remember is that Google cannot be tricked via SEO.

CONCLUSION

Indeed, this book has guided you a step by step to making your own unique blog. After you adhere to all guidelines in this book, I promise you that making money at home is that easy and no limit to how you much money you can earn as long as you stand out to be unique.

Blogging is a fun, often addictive, and extremely rewarding activity on many levels. The luckiest and most hardworking bloggers have discovered how to earn a living doing nothing but creating, producing, managing, and promoting their blog.

Countless others have found ways to incorporate a blog into their personal or professional lives, and at the same time, generate a small, but steady stream of revenue from it.

Meanwhile, some people use blogging as a powerful sales, marketing, public relations, or promotional tool for themselves, a company, a product, or a service.

It's no secret that everyone would like to get paid for doing what they love. If you have a passion for blogging, the secret you need to uncover is how to generate revenue from it so your blog transforms from a fun hobby into a lucrative business venture.

As you'll discover, blogging is a great way to earn some money while writing about the topic(s) you're truly passionate about. However, blogging is not a get-rich-quick scheme or a guaranteed moneymaker.

If you do wind up earning a significant amount of revenue as a direct result of blogging, it will be because of your hard work, passion, dedication, and the significant time you invest into promoting your blog by taking a multifaceted approach to building an audience for it.